PETS

Julie Ashworth   John Clark

CollinsELT

A Division of HarperCollinsPublishers

CONTENTS

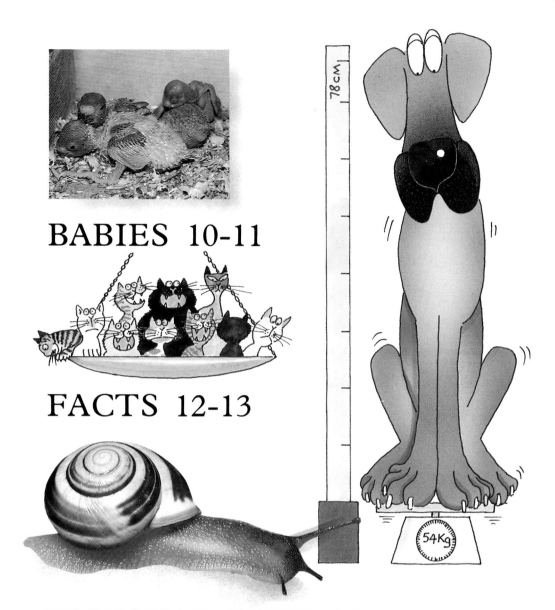

PETS

What is a pet?
A pet is an animal. It lives in
your home. These animals are pets.

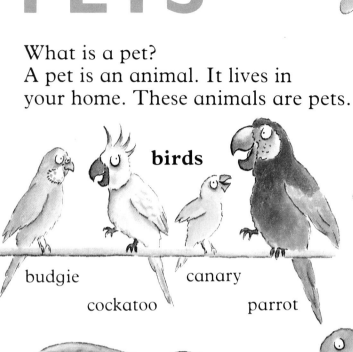

dog

birds

budgie

cockatoo

canary

parrot

mouse

snake

tortoise

rat

fish

hamster

goldfish

tropical fish

gerbil

guinea-pig

cat

rabbit

4

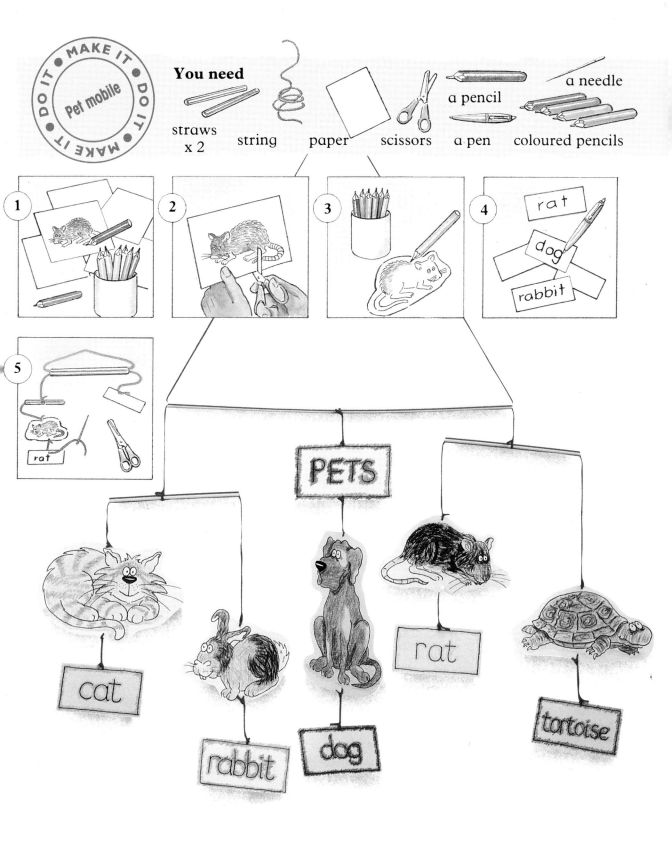

MAKE IT • DO IT
DO IT • MAKE IT
Pet mobile

You need

straws x 2   string   paper   scissors   a pencil   a pen   coloured pencils   a needle

1

2

3

4

rat

dog

rabbit

5

rat

PETS

cat

rabbit

dog

rat

tortoise

PET CARE

Pets need a home

kennel

basket

cage

hutch

tank

box

things to eat and drink   and things to play with.

You need

a box   paper   pebbles   shells   a pencil   tape   scissors   paint   a paintbrush   string   a needle

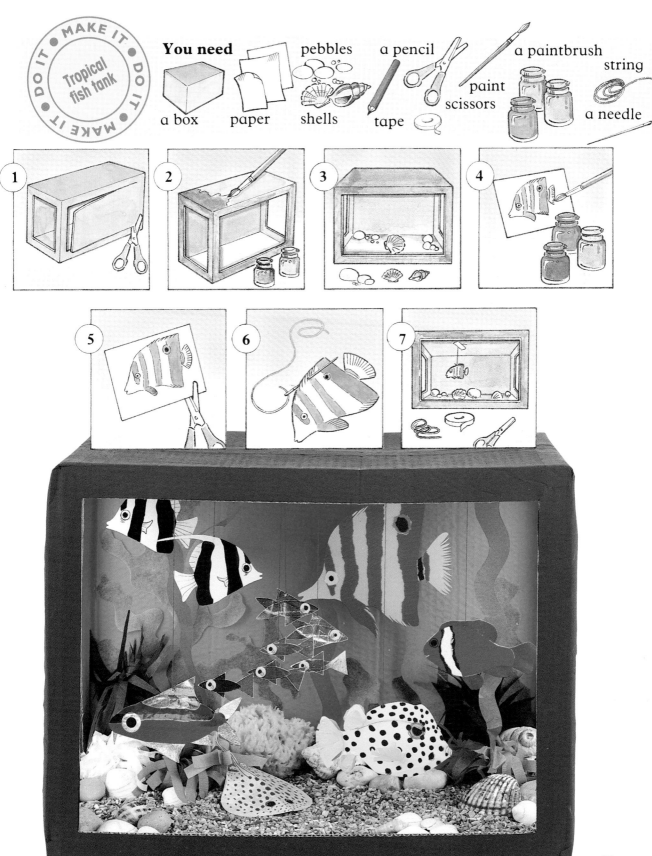

7

APPEARANCE

short ears

long ears

fur

whiskers

fur

short tail

paw

claws

paw

nose

feathers

wings

long tail

hard shell

beak

claws

Colours

fin

black and white

tail

long tail

orange

blue

yellow

red

You need

 a photo   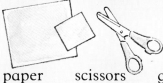 paper   scissors   glue   a pen   coloured pencils

My Pet : Hercules

ears

big black eyes

brown and white fur

small nose

whiskers

short legs

home

toys

food

HAMSTER MIX

Kim Choc. Treats

PASSPORT	
NAME	Hercules
ANIMAL	hamster
AGE	one year
COLOUR	brown and white
SIZE	small

BABIES

A baby dog is called a **puppy**.

One week   One month   Three months

A baby cat is called a **kitten**.

One day   Three weeks   Ten weeks

A baby bird is called a **chick**.

Four days   Three weeks   One year

FACTS

The fattest cat in the world was called Himmy.

He weighed 20.7 kg. Normal cats weigh about 2 kg.

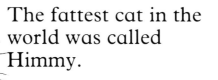

Cats sleep about 16 hours every day!

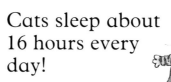

The biggest dog in the world is a St Bernard.

78 cm

The tallest dog is a Great Dane.

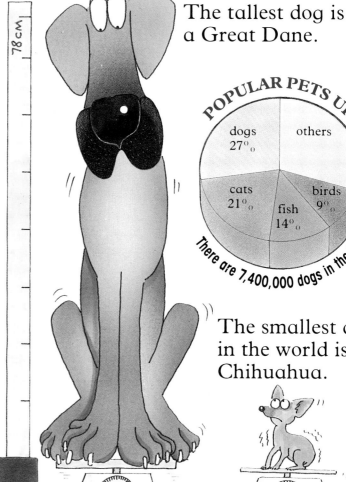

POPULAR PETS UK

dogs 27%

others

cats 21%

fish 14%

birds 9%

There are 7,400,000 dogs in the UK!

The smallest dog in the world is a Chihuahua.

100Kg

54Kg

1·5kg

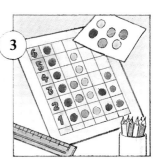

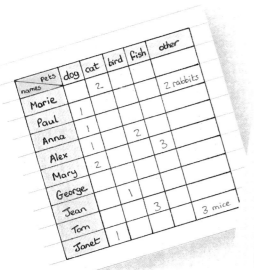

pets names	dog	cat	bird	fish	other
Marie		2			2 rabbits
Paul	1				
Anna	1		2		
Alex				3	
Mary	2				
George			1		
Jean				3	3 mice
Tom					
Janet	1				

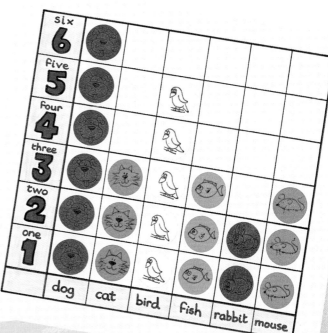

	dog	cat	bird	fish	rabbit	mouse

13

UNUSUAL PETS

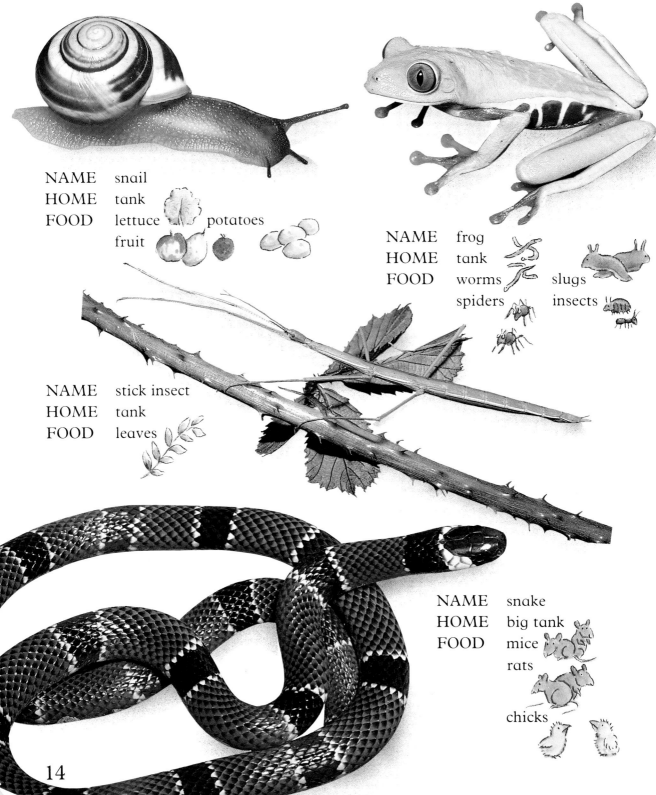

NAME   snail
HOME   tank
FOOD   lettuce   potatoes
        fruit

NAME   frog
HOME   tank
FOOD   worms   slugs
        spiders   insects

NAME   stick insect
HOME   tank
FOOD   leaves

NAME   snake
HOME   big tank
FOOD   mice
        rats

        chicks

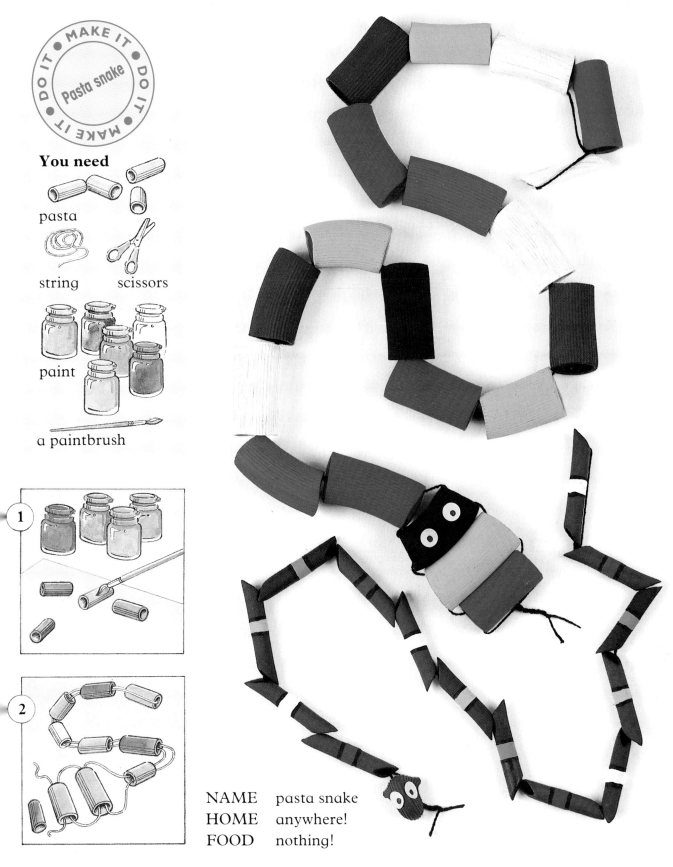

Pasta snake

You need

pasta

string   scissors

paint

a paintbrush

1

2

NAME   pasta snake
HOME   anywhere!
FOOD   nothing!

15

SOUNDS

What do pets say?

UK	woof
France	ouha ouha
Italy	bau bau
Japan	wan wan
Spain	guau guau

meow	UK
miaou	France
miao	Italy
nyan nyan	Japan
miau-miau	Spain

MAKE IT • DO IT • MAKE IT • DO IT

Pet tape

You need

a tape recorder

a tape